EARLY GRACE WITH EARLY GLORY.

A Brief Memorial

OF

A BELOVED DAUGHTER.

BY THE

REV. W. P. LYON, B.A.,

TUNBRIDGE WELLS.

LONDON:

WARD & CO., 27, PATERNOSTER ROW.

EDINBURGH: T. C. JACK, 92, PRINCES STREET.

TUNBRIDGE WELLS: A. SYME, PARADE.

PRICE SIXPENCE.

EARLY GRACE WITH EARLY GLORY.

A

𝔅rief 𝔐emorial

OF

A BELOVED DAUGHTER.

BY THE

REV. W. P. LYON, B.A.
TUNBRIDGE WELLS.

LONDON:
WARD & CO., 27, PATERNOSTER ROW.
EDINBURGH: THOMAS C. JACK, 92, PRINCES-STREET.
TUNBRIDGE WELLS: A. SYME, PARADE.

LONDON:
REED AND PARDON, PRINTERS,
PATERNOSTER ROW.

EARLY GRACE WITH EARLY GLORY.

JANE JOANNA LYON, the subject of this Memoir, was the second surviving child of the Rev. W. P. Lyon. She was born in London on the 3rd of May, 1843, and died at Tunbridge Wells, on the 18th of November, 1854. The earthly course of this dear child was thus a short one, extending only to eleven years and six months. But though thus short, it disclosed a character which not only endeared her to all who knew her, but also gave them satisfying evidence that Divine grace had been training her for a purer and brighter world. In the little circle in which she moved her path was indeed like the shining light, and serene and lovely was the ray which shone from it. From her earliest years she seems to have been a genuine subject of the kingdom of heaven. Though doubtless a sharer in the original corruption of our nature, she yet appears at a very early age to have had her heart moulded by renewing grace. There was never manifested in her any disposition to turn away from the pure light of the Sun of Righteousness. She learned in the very dawn of life to love that light; and she continued to walk in it, and rejoice in it, as it shone around her with growing brightness, till she reached the perfect day of heaven.

This short account of her has been prepared with the desire of retaining as distinct an image of her as possible before the minds of those most nearly connected with her, and with the hope that, while it cannot fail to be interesting to them, it may not be altogether unprofitable to others.

TRAINING OF THE OPENING MIND.

When an infant, Janie was dedicated by her parents to God. A devoted missionary of the cross, then on a visit to this country, and well known for his long and arduous labours among the heathen—the Rev. A. F. Lacroix, of Calcutta—administered to her the ordinance of baptism, and thus received her as a disciple into the school of Christ. Many fervent prayers were then offered that she might become in early life one of the lambs of the fold of Jesus, and evidence was soon given that these prayers were neither unheard nor unanswered.

As her mind began to open, she was instructed from the word of God. Short stories from the Bible were selected, to hear which, she, with her brothers and sisters, assembled at stated times around their parents. It was pleasing to observe how soon they engaged the attention of Janie, and touched her heart. From its shorter stories she passed to its more extended narratives and parables, and thus, from the lives of Scripture characters, and from the pictures of divine truths drawn by the pen of inspiration, she gathered, when very young, a knowledge of her fallen condition as a sinner, and of the way of salvation through Jesus Christ.

It was soon evident that no book could have been chosen so well fitted as the Bible to engage and interest the mind even of a child. Where can narratives be found more full of touching interest and thrilling tenderness than those of Joseph and Moses, of Samuel and Timothy? Where have we records of more instructive events than in the histories of Abel and Abraham, of David and Daniel, and of the apostles of our Lord and Saviour? Where can a child be brought into contact with so much that is pure and lovely, and so fitted to draw out and hallow the best tendencies of our nature, as when led to follow the footsteps of the Saviour as he treads his lowly pathway through life; to gaze on his wonderful works; to accompany him on his visits of mercy; to see him amid his sorrows in the garden and on the cross, and when lying cold, and stiff, and lifeless, in the grave; and then to behold him on the morning of his resurrection, when angels roll away the stone from the door of his sepulchre, when he shakes off the sleep of death as one would the slumbers of a night, and comes forth no more to die? Subjects like these never lose their interest and freshness. They cannot be brought before the mind even of a child, in a suitable way, without awakening the deepest and purest feelings, checking the budding evil, and strengthening the latent good, and proving a well-spring of the holiest and healthiest influences.

As soon as Janie was able to express herself she was taught to pray. At first she would repeat the words which were given her. After a time she was gradually led to give utterance to her feelings and desires in her own language; and then she was encouraged to retire, that she might seek intercourse with God. There is reason to believe that from the time she was able to understand the nature of prayer she was regularly in the practice, every morning and evening at least, of being alone, that she might draw near to God. If children, in being taught to pray, were led to express in it the feelings and sentiments of their own hearts as soon as they become capable of uttering them, and to regard themselves as speaking directly to a loving Saviour, it would prove to them a more interesting and delightful occupation. Everything of course depends on the Divine blessing. The most suitable means, however, for awakening and interesting the mind should not be overlooked. The Divine Spirit works by instruments, and cannot be expected to make use of such as are unfit for the work to be done. Let it not be thought then that anything is good enough for children. Their characters and dispositions must be kept in view, and those means employed which are most suited rightly to influence them. Attention to this is all the more necessary in connection with prayer, from the natural disinclination of the heart to this heavenly engagement.

DEVELOPMENT OF CHARACTER.

Janie was naturally amiable. Her heart was warm and affectionate, and as she grew up she manifested the most engaging and lovely dispositions. She could not indeed give her affections and confidence to every one. Her strong attachments were few, and were formed with great discrimination. But where she did love, she loved intensely and with her whole heart. As to intellectual qualities, she did not perhaps possess to any great extent such as are brilliant and shining; but she had for her years remarkable maturity of mind and soundness of judgment, along with great power of application and industry. She was also very lively and cheerful, and had a considerable fund of humour, which rendered her a most interesting companion.

It was at home, however, that she was best known, and that the lovely features of her character were most strikingly manifested. To her parents she was a most affectionate and dutiful child, and could not bear to be under their displeasure. Rare indeed were the occasions when they had to reprove her. She was always ready and cheerful in her obedience, transparent and truthful in her conduct, and was remarkable

for a thoughtfulness which was ever leading
her, unasked, to do for those around her
what she thought might be helpful. She
loved her brothers and sisters ardently, and
had great influence with them. They were,
with one exception, younger than herself;
and she had succeeded, by her affectionate
kindness and gentle firmness, in so attach-
ing them to her, that she was among the
last they would have ventured to offend. A
word or even a look from her was generally
sufficient either to restrain or encourage
them. She knew well, moreover, how to
interest and occupy them, and took great
delight in having them under her charge.
Her parents always felt that if Janie was
with them, whether within doors or without,
all was well.

This influence with children was not con-
fined to her own home circle. One who
had seen much of her says, in a letter to
her parents: "She was characterized by
much benevolence and kindness. This was
beautifully manifested in her love for little
children, and in the delight she took in im-
parting instruction to them. Weight of
character may seem a strange quality to at-
tribute to one so young; but I know not
by what other term to designate that mar-
vellous influence so discreetly used by her,

through which she could sway a whole circle of juveniles, without assuming any undue authority, and which often enabled her to keep them for a length of time happy and pleased."

Till her last illness began Janie had been a strong and healthy child. No one who looked on her blooming countenance and well-knit frame, who saw her firm step and bright eye, or heard her merry laugh, could ever have imagined that her course on earth was to be so brief. Her friends anticipated that her life would be prolonged, and great pains were taken to qualify her for a course of activity and usefulness.

EDUCATION.

Janie's educational advantages were very considerable, and most diligently did she improve them. She was industrious both at home and at school. It was rarely she neglected her lessons; and if at any time she did relax, she soon made up for it by renewed earnestness and application.

The winter of 1852-3 she spent in Edinburgh. Her aunt, to whose care she was entrusted, says regarding her, "On one occasion, being detained at school longer than usual, she came home weeping bitterly, and put a note into my hand from the teacher, explaining that she had been detained to learn her lesson more perfectly. This seemed to give her so much distress that she took care it never occurred again."

But her education was received chiefly at the establishment of an excellent friend at Tunbridge Wells, Miss Billing, who bears the following testimony to her character. " In forming an estimate (she says) of your dear child from her school career, reference must be had to her habitual course. This was uniformly gentle, quiet, affectionate, respectful, obedient, and persevering. She was punctual and diligent in her studies, and by steady thoughtfulness and a habit of reflecting on what she was taught, her apprehension of subjects was unusually clear. Her composition consequently showed the power of her mind. In everything she was characterized by carefulness and exactness. Always reverential when reading the Scriptures, she evinced a marked and growing seriousness and fixed attention during the last few months. I often thought she appeared to be reflecting and settling in her own mind something connected with the reading; and when I would remark (as sometimes I did), ' Such a thing is worthy of notice,' or 'You would do well to treasure up this for some opportunity of teaching it to others in a Sunday-school, or to your little brothers and sisters at home,' she would look up with particular interest, and now and then venture to ask a question or make a reply.

"I remember only one instance in which she incurred reproof; but this was followed by such deep and sincere penitence, that I have no doubt her application by faith to the Saviour's blood was effectual in cleansing the stain away. Indeed, the absence of evil in one so young, except enough to identify her with the fallen family which the Saviour died to redeem, together with the interest and delight she so evidently felt in the things of God, are to my mind most satisfactory evidences of her having been a subject of renewing grace."

"Persevering industry and diligence (says her aunt, whose letter has been already quoted,) were prominent features in her character. I can yet see her earnest, thoughtful countenance, poring over a difficult lesson, studiously examining a map, or intent upon some intricate piece of needlework. She was very orderly in her habits, and showed that love of neatness and tidiness which generally marks a refined and well-regulated mind."

LOVE OF NEATNESS AND ORDER.

This trait of her character is worthy of notice. After her removal everything belonging to her was found in perfect order. Her work-box, writing-desk, &c., were carefully arranged. There was no confusion. The different articles were neatly laid aside. Everything was in its place. Her writing displayed the same qualities. It was remarkably clear and distinct. Even the punctuation was carefully attended to. Her copybooks rarely exhibited a blot. On leaving school at the midsummer holidays, she put her school books together in a place by themselves, to be ready for future use. Little did she think then that she should never open them again. But so was it ordered. The *last* lesson had been learned, the *last* exercise written ; and now she must enter the school of affliction, there to be disciplined and prepared for the higher and holier employments of heaven.

DELIGHT IN NATURE.

The works of God in the world of nature around her were a source of deep and never-failing pleasure to this much-loved child.

C

She delighted in country walks, in the gathering of wild flowers, and in observing the habits of the different tribes of the animal creation. The knowledge which in this way she acquired was remarkable in one so young. The following extract from a letter written by her when ten years of age to a younger brother, will show her power of observation, and her delight in nature. She was then on a visit with her uncle and aunt to the Bridge of Allan, near Stirling.

" Yesterday I went to see Castle Campbell, the Devil's Mill, the Rumbling Bridge, and last and best, the Caldron Lynn. Castle Campbell is an old ruin, but we could not get at it, as there was a deep valley and a river between us and it. The Devil's Mill is a precipice, with the river Devon falling over it. The water makes a sound like a mill, and it is called the Devil's Mill because it is always at work. The Rumbling Bridge is a very narrow bridge, but although it is so narrow, horses and carts used to pass over it. I should tell you that there was no wall or fence of any kind to keep them from falling into the deep, deep water below. The water, as it rushes along among the rocks, makes a rumbling sound, and from that the bridge gets its name. But now for the Caldron Lynn. You know a *caldron* is just a *pot*. Well, we went to see it, and it is *so* like a pot, with water boiling in it. There are two cascades, but the last one was so pretty. It was a precipice, forty-four feet high, with the river pouring over it, and sending up the spray into the air; and as the sun was shining on it, it made a rainbow on one side of it. It looked very grand and beautiful, and as aunt and I sat admiring it, we wished you had been with us."

She was also much interested in conchology, and had made considerable progress in the study of it. A collection of shells, which she had made with great care, and arranged with remarkable neatness and order, remains behind as a pleasing memorial of her partiality to this branch of knowledge.

INDICATIONS OF PIETY.

But our object in writing this brief memoir is chiefly to direct attention to those indications of piety which appeared in Janie from her earliest years, and which shone with such a pure and genial ray through the whole of her brief career. We have already noticed her love to the Word of God. The Bible had been her chief lesson-book, and many happy hours did she spend in the study of it. Very delightful to her were the occasions when the little family group was gathered for the purpose of searching the inspired volume, and asking and answering questions which it suggested. Her delight in it was pleasingly manifested in the following incident, which occurred shortly before her death. One afternoon, her mother went into her bed-room where she had lain quiet for more than an hour. She said with a sweet smile, " I have not slept, but I have been quite comfortable. I was thinking of dear Miss B.'s Bible-class, and how happy we used to be there. I have thought too of an exercise for W. on Sabbath afternoons. Let him take the letters of the alphabet, and find out a place mentioned in the Bible beginning with each of the letters. He should take A to begin with, describe the place, and tell anything remarkable that happened there. Then let him take B, then C, and so on through the alphabet. I will give him the first three." She then mentioned—Asphaltites, (the Dead Sea), Bethlehem, and Calvary. The writing of short essays on Scripture subjects was a favourite occupation with her during the leisure hours of the Sabbath. Several of these still remain, some of them showing considerable research. Among others, there are " Proofs from the Old Testament of God's hatred to sin:" " Joseph a type of Christ:" " Description of the Valley of Hinnom:" and " Remarkable events connected with the river Jordan." The 14th chapter of St. John, the 23rd Psalm, and those chapters in Revelation which describe the glories of the New Jerusalem, were favourite portions of Scripture with her. She frequently alluded to them, and during her illness derived from them much comfort and enjoyment.

Janie had learned, moreover, the value and the power of prayer. It has been already stated that her parents have reason to believe, that, from a very early age, she was accustomed regularly to retire alone, that she might draw near to God. Prayer was not with her a mere formal exercise which she was glad to get over, but a source of strength and a well-spring of pleasure. This will appear from the following incidents, which are selected from among others.

For some time her mother had been in the habit of taking her and her elder sister alone for a few minutes, just before they started for school in the morning. This was for the purpose of commending them to the care of the Heavenly Shepherd. Janie was always ready for this engagement, and if at any time it was omitted, her disappointment was very apparent. On resuming her duties at school, after her return from Scotland, she came one morning to her mother, and said with much earnestness, " Mamma, do you remember what you used to do just before we left for school ? I wish you would do so again." On the occasion already referred to, when she went for the winter to Edinburgh, her feeling with reference to prayer was strikingly manifested. Leaving home was a great trial to her. Her affectionate heart could hardly bear it. A short time before the hour of separation she came seeking her mother, saying, " Mamma, will you pray with me, and ask God to give me strength to go away ?"

She took great delight in religious conversation. " Often, (says her aunt), when talking with her on the sinfulness of her nature, and the necessity of a change of heart, she has sat on my lap and wept for a considerable time, and would frequently ask me on such occasions to pray with her." How beautifully did this indicate a mind struggling with its natural evil and infirmity, and seeking to rise from it into a higher sphere, where God might be found and enjoyed !

We might notice also the interest manifested by her in the spread of religion. She regularly perused the Juvenile Missionary Magazine, and assisted the blessed cause of missions by needlework, as well as by cheerfully contributing to it from her little store. "For a whole year (says her aunt), while with us, she voluntarily abstained from the use of butter, that she might have a small weekly allowance for her missionary box. This box was also regularly placed by her on the breakfast-table every Sabbath morning, to receive the contributions of her friends." A small sum of money, given her by a kind friend, she appropriated for the repair of the missionary ship. She took a special interest in this vessel, and was greatly delighted by the accounts of its voyages.

To this it may be added, that frequently on her way to school she would take with her a parcel of little tracts for children, and accost any she happened to meet. She always took care to ascertain whether the child to whom she offered a tract could read, and if answered in the affirmative, she would say, with a kind look or approving smile, "Now, you can take it home, and read it to your mother." One Sabbath-day her attention was arrested by two little girls, who, at

the time of divine service, were evidently
not going in the direction of a place of
worship. She went up to them with the
inquiry, "Where are you going?" "Home,"
said one of the children. "Oh!" she replied, "you should not go home yet, come
with me to the house of God: you do not
know how nice it is to go there." The
children yielded, and before taking her accustomed place, she had the satisfaction of
seeing her two little protégées accommo-
dated with seats.

ILLNESS AND DEATH.

At length the time came when this beloved child was to be removed to a happier
world. Disease, however, approached her
very stealthily. Indeed, so gently did it lay
its hand on her, that it was difficult for her
friends at first to imagine there was any
danger. They could hardly bring themselves to believe that one who had been so
blooming and healthy, and who was appa-
rently so fitted for life, was so soon to resign
it. But disease had in truth laid upon her
an unyielding hold, and under its influence
she gradually wasted away. The colour
disappeared from her cheeks; the strength

fled from her limbs; every thing that medical skill and kindness could suggest was done to arrest the progress of the distemper, but in vain. It steadily advanced, notwithstanding every care, and after a while it became evident, even to herself, that the issue would be fatal. She had long been aware that her case was a doubtful one, but she was not afraid to die. She more than once expressed her willingness to depart, and to be with Christ. When her father informed her a few days before her death that there was positively no hope, no possibility of recovery, she received the intimation with the most perfect calmness. On a former occasion, when a similar intimation had been given her, a solitary tear stole into her eye, which she immediately brushed away. But on this occasion no tear was shed, and no alarm expressed. The sting of death had been taken away, and she could lie in calm and happy repose on the bosom of the Saviour whom she loved.

The following incidents connected with her illness will help a little more fully to illustrate her character. It had been arranged that early in July, Janie, with the other members of the family, should pay a visit to the beloved relations in Edinburgh under whose roof she formerly resided. This

visit had been long looked forward to, and
from it she anticipated great enjoyment.
A few days before the period fixed for de-
parture, the dear child became worse, and
medical opinion was unfavourable to her
leaving home. In these circumstances it
was resolved that she should remain with
her mother, while the others went. This
was a painful trial, and with much anxiety
and fear her mother communicated to her
the disappointment of her hopes. For a
little time she wept bitterly. By-and-by,
however, recovering her composure, she said,
" Well, I shall have *you* with me, and if I
do not feel better than I am now, I could not
enjoy even a visit to Edinburgh." In allu-
sion to this trial she was asked, " Do you
not feel it hard to be ill, and unable to
enjoy life as you see other children doing ? "
She said, " No, I think God has been very
kind in sending this illness ; it is to make
me think more about heaven."

One Sabbath evening her mother asked
her, " Do you really love Jesus ? " " Yes, oh,
yes," she replied, " but not half enough. I
have not mourned over my sins as many do,
and I fear I have never been sorry enough
about them." She was reminded that it
was not her *feelings* that would save her,
but only Jesus, whose blood could cleanse

from all sin. She was then asked if she felt sin to be hateful, and if she wished to be free from it? "Yes, indeed, I do," she replied. "Can you remember," she was asked again, "any instance mentioned in Scripture of one who was brought to love and serve Jesus without the distressing convictions of sin that some experience?" She said, "I think that in the Ethiopian eunuch we have such an instance; also in Lydia. Paul was an instance of the opposite kind." On this occasion she seemed in an elevated and rejoicing state of mind. After being laid to rest, she was heard singing—

> "Begone, unbelief, my Saviour is near,
>   And for my relief will surely appear;
>   By prayer let me wrestle, and he will perform;
>   With Christ in the vessel, I smile at the storm."

On another Sabbath she said to her mother, "I was so happy while you were at chapel. The house was quiet, and I was able to feel that Jesus was with me. He kept Satan from troubling me with wandering thoughts, and I felt so happy." She was asked what she had been thinking about? "I thought of the love of Jesus," she said, "and pictured him to myself as hanging on the cross, that it might help me to love him more." Her mother remarked that many of

God's people had been praying for her, and asking that Jesus would be with her to cheer her with his presence, now that she was unable to seek him in the house of prayer. "Yes," she said, "others may have been praying for me; but perhaps if I had not prayed *myself*, Jesus would not have come to me."

Sending a message one day to her much-loved relative in Edinburgh, she said, "You may tell aunt that I am almost sure I love Jesus. I asked him to help me to open the door of my heart, and I think he has helped me." The inquiry was then made, "How do you ask him?" She replied, "I put him in mind of his promises, and beg of him to fulfil them." "What promises?" "I love them that love me, and they that seek me early shall find me;" and "Him that cometh unto me I will in no wise cast out." "Could you willingly give up your beloved relatives, and go to Jesus if it were His will?" She said, "Yes; for since this illness came on, I do not feel much enjoyment in what used to please me, and I do not think it would be difficult for me to give you all up."

One day she said, "What an awful thing it would be if I were to deceive myself, and think that I loved Jesus when I did not."

Her mother replied, " Are you willing that God should search your heart, and show you the evil that may be in it?" "Oh, yes," she said, "I am." David's words seemed much to interest her, "Search me, O God, and know my heart; try me, and know my thoughts; and see if there be any wicked way in me, and lead me in the way everlasting." After conversing some time she said, "Pray for me that I may not be deceived."

One evening when alone with her mother, the conversation turned upon the earnest desire felt by her parents for the early conversion of their children. She suddenly looked up and said, "Why are you so anxious, mamma?" "Surely," it was replied, "you can answer that question yourself." She said, "Perhaps I could, but I should like you to tell me."

Some remarks were then made about the value of the soul, and the love of Christ in dying to save sinners. "Is it wonderful, then," she was asked, "that we wish to know how you feel towards such a Saviour?" She said, "Do you remember an anecdote we heard in a sermon lately? A woman came to a minister, and said she had long been praying for the conversion of her husband, but as yet her prayers had not been

D

answered. He asked her what her chief motive was for desiring the conversion of her husband? 'Oh!' she said, 'it would make us all so happy! our home would be so delightful! it would be like a new world!' The minister said, 'If your motive for asking is your own happiness, and not the glory of God, you need not wonder that your prayers remain unanswered.'" The dear child evidently wished that her parents, in seeking the conversion of their children, should be influenced, not by mere natural affection, but by the highest of all motives, desire for the glory of God.[1]

The calmness and serenity of mind exhibited by her as her illness advanced, were beheld with wonder and with praise. Naturally timid, and apt to shrink from separation from those she fondly loved, she was enabled to triumph over natural feeling, and without a murmur or a tear peacefully to wait the coming of her Lord. She suffered but little except from the weakness which accompanied the decay and exhaustion of the body. The path by which she descended to the grave declined very gently, and she trod it most meekly and patiently. Death came to her at last very suddenly, but without violence or pain. Her parents were with her at the time. She seemed to feel uncomfortable, and asked to be raised. She was raised on her mother's arm. For a moment an unearthly brightness glanced from the eye, as if it was piercing into eternity. The breathing instantly ceased, and all was over. Without a struggle, or even a sigh, her ransomed spirit passed away to be for ever with the Lord.

Thus gently and peacefully did this dear child exchange earth for heaven, and the society of sorrowing friends for that of rejoicing angels and the spirits of the just made perfect. Ere those who loved her so much knew that she was gone, or she herself had time to bid them farewell, she found herself in that bright world for which divine grace had prepared her, and had done with sin and sorrow for ever. Very fragrant is the memory she has left behind, and long will it be cherished as a precious legacy by those who now sorrow for her, though not without a most bright and cheering hope. They can think of her as now in the presence of that Saviour whom she loved, as sinless and happy before his throne, as devoting her immortal powers to his service, and as helping to swell those songs of triumphant gratitude which re-echo in the temple of heaven. They can look forward also to that time when Christ, who is her life, shall appear, and when she shall appear with him in glory; the vile body being fashioned by him like unto his glorious body, according to the working whereby he is able even to subdue all things unto himself.

CONCLUDING REFLECTIONS.

But does not the brief career of this dear departed one read some important lessons to survivors? It shows, for one thing, *the pleasantness of true religion.* Janie may be said to have been influenced by it from her earliest years. It shed its hallowed influence around her when she was very young. And never did she withdraw herself from it. Few lives so short have passed more happily than hers. She was naturally cheerful, and much did she enjoy the brief span of earthly existence that was allotted to her. While she would have shrunk with instinctive dread from anything that was sinful, she could enter with keen relish into every innocent and healthful pleasure. The happiness of some people is of such a kind that it passes away the moment religion appears. If *they* are to be cheerful and joyous, the name of God must not be mentioned. Jesus must not be spoken of. There must be no reference to eternal things. Their happiness cannot consist with the remembrance of such subjects. They can be happy only when they are forgetting God, and banishing from their minds everything that most deserves consideration. But this is not true happiness. A happiness that cannot live in the light of divine truth is not worthy of the name. It was otherwise with the subject of this Memoir. Her happiest hours were those in which the light of God and of the Lamb shone most brightly around her. She walked in it through life. It was the shining of it in her sick chamber that kept her mind so peaceful and happy; and sure we are that she now rejoices in that light as it shines on her more bright and clear in that city which needs no sun and no moon to illumine it, because it is lighted up by the glory of God and of the Lamb.

Let the youthful readers of this little narrative, then, put away from them the thought that the religion of Jesus is full of melancholy and gloom. It is only they who do not know it who can imagine this. Those who have tried it know that the reverse is the fact. They find it giving them a purer and sweeter happiness than they ever tasted

D 2

before. It leads them to the river of God's pleasures. It becomes in them a well of water springing up into a life of heavenly peace and satisfying enjoyment. It sanctifies their minds. It purifies their hearts. It refines their pleasures. It leads them to lives of true usefulness. It elevates and blesses their whole nature, and prepares them for that world in which Christ is seen as he is, where his people are like him, and where he himself shall lead them to the living fountains of water.

And is there aught that tends to melancholy in this? Is it a gloomy thing to have sin forgiven, to have the conscience brought to peace, to have the heart influenced by love to Christ, to have the fear of death taken away, and the hope of heaven cheering and gladdening the heart? Is that person unhappy who can say of God, "He is my Father;" of Jesus, "He is my Saviour;" of the Holy Spirit, "He is my Sanctifier and Comforter;" and of heaven, "It will be my happy and everlasting home?" Surely there is nothing here that tends to gloom, but everything to fill the mind with cheerfulness and joy. On the other hand, they cannot be regarded as otherwise than truly miserable who turn away from such subjects with dislike; who have no love to Christ, can find no delight in God, and who, in the prospects of the Christian, can see no beauty that they should desire them.

We trust that the youthful readers of this Memoir will be convinced by it at least of this one thing — that wisdom's ways are pleasantness, and that all her paths are peace. Let them be persuaded to choose those ways in early life. Let them begin, while yet young, to tread those paths of peace. They will infallibly lead them to useful and happy lives on earth, prepare them for peaceful and it may be triumphant deaths, and for a glorious immortality.

Christian parents may learn from this Memoir that *there is no reason why they should not expect their prayers and efforts for the spiritual good of their children to result in their conversion to God, even when they are very young.* Why should they not be under the influence of the Spirit from their earliest years? Why should they not, like John the Baptist, be filled with the Holy Ghost from life's first dawn? Why should they not resemble Timothy, who from a child knew the Holy Scriptures, which are able to make wise unto salvation? Why should they not, like Samuel, be chosen by God for his service, and have the high privilege of entering upon it in the opening morning of their days? Are there not made to Christian parents in the word of God many exceeding great and gracious promises? May they not hear God saying to them, regarding each little one committed to their charge, "Take this child, and nurse it for me?" May they not regard the words in which Jehovah once spake to Abraham as addressed by him also to themselves—"I will be a God to thee, and to thy seed after thee?" Did not Jesus confirm this gracious promise when he said, "Suffer the little children to come unto me, and forbid them not, for of such is the kingdom of heaven?" Little children are reckoned as subjects of this kingdom; and not unless, on growing up, they throw off its restraints, and rebel against its authority, shall they be excluded from its blessedness.

Parents, therefore, should regard their little ones as subjects of the heavenly King. They should teach them, from their earliest years, to look up to Jesus not only as their Saviour, but also as their Sovereign, whom they are bound to love, and honour, and obey. They should instruct them in the truths relating to his character and kingdom, and endeavour by every possible means to bring them under their influence.

The Sabbath should be made a happy day to them—the best of all the seven. There are abundant means, through the divine blessing, of accomplishing this. Only let the minds of the children be occupied with what is fitted to instruct and interest them. Let them be led, as they are able, to use their mental powers. When a chapter is read, let them be encouraged to ask questions regarding its contents. When a Scripture place or character is selected as an exercise, let them one after another mention any fact they may remember regarding it. Let such of them as are sufficiently advanced for it be induced to write short and simple papers on such subjects. Let them be drawn to such engagements by the cords of love. Let everything like *tasking* or *forcing* them be avoided. A little care, and effort, and kindness, would render such occupations truly delightful to them, while they could not fail to be instructive and profitable. The hours of the Sabbath would thus pass pleasantly away, and the day, when it closes, be felt by them to have been but too short. Scripture prints and maps, Bible stories and biographies, religious anecdotes, and brief memoirs of youthful Christians, will afford valuable aid in this interesting and delightful work.

But it must be superintended by the
parents themselves. On no account should
it be delegated to others. In the spirit of
love, and patience, and prayer, they should
persevere in it. Their responsibility must
be kept in view, and the divine command
be ever before them, "Provoke not your
children to wrath, but bring them up in the
nurture and admonition of the Lord," Eph.
vi. 4. "And these words, which I command
thee this day, shall be in thine heart: and
thou shalt teach them diligently unto thy
children, and shalt talk of them when thou
sittest in thine house, and when thou walk-
est by the way, and when thou liest down,
and when thou risest up," Deut. vi. 6, 7.
The injunction should not be forgotten,
"Train up a child in the way he should
go;" nor should the encouraging promise
be overlooked, "When he is old, he will not
depart from it," Prov. xxii. 6.

Were parents but more earnest and be-
lieving in prayer for their children, and
more diligent and patient in effort to train
them for God, they would be more success-
ful. What! has God promised, and will
he not perform? Will he be unfaithful
to his word? Put away the unbelieving
thought. Oh, Christian parent, labour on
in faith and hope; in the spirit of love, and

patience, and fidelity. Let the love of Christ be your motive, and the glory of God your end. In due season you shall reap if you faint not. Do not be discouraged if the seed you sow does not immediately spring up. " Behold, the husbandman waiteth for the precious fruit of the earth, and hath long patience for it, until he receive the early and latter rain." Your labour meanwhile is not overlooked. There is One who says, " I know thy works, and thy labour, and thy patience." Yield not then to discouragement. Give not way to despondency. "In the morning sow thy seed, and in the evening withhold not thine hand." For, " He that goeth forth and weepeth, bearing precious seed, shall doubtless come again with rejoicing, bringing his sheaves with him."

Reed and Pardon, Printers, Paternoster Row, London.

Preparing for Publication,

THE MEDIATORIAL KINGDOM OF CHRIST,

IN RELATION TO

HIS SECOND ADVENT.